"Every now and then, we all need to take time to reflect on our lives. It grounds us and gives us hope. In this book, *You're Something Special*, Dr. Ross and Carol Hall provide that opportunity to reexamine some truths so we can live life to the fullest! You will enjoy it!"

—ROB WOODARD, Colorado State Senator
Loveland, Colo.

Thank you, Ron and Carol, for reminding us we are truly special ... that only in God through Christ can we answer life's greatest questions: Who am I? Why am I here? Where am I going? This is a must-read for all seekers of true meaning and fulfillment!"

—JOHNNY HALL, One Voice Mission
Colorado Springs, Colo.

"This is a book I so desire my grandchildren to read!"

—PASTOR KC BEDUNNAH, Pastor
Council Bluffs, Iowa

"Whether you're used to hearing these three uplifting words, *You're Something Special*, or you've rarely heard them, I strongly encourage you to read this book. Then share this book and these three words with those you love. You'll be glad you did!"

—DAVE CORNELL, Author, Speaker
Fergus Falls, Minn.

"My Grandfather certainly has a way with words and is excellent at getting people to think. This book shares the light he so faithfully radiates in his everyday life. *You're Something Special* is a wonderful book. Pick it up — you will surely be blessed."

—RICKY ARNEL, Pastor
Port St. Lucie, Fla.

"How much more peace and purpose would we have within our lives if we would accept the uniqueness with which God has designed each of us? *You're Something Special* will hit you on a deep and heartfelt level as you enter into a greater understanding of the timeless truth that God is forever for you!"

—SCOTT BECKENHAUER, Pastor
Omaha, Nebr.

"A perfect template for understanding why we are something special, this book shows a true path to becoming all we were meant to be. The constant reminder that we all need a spiritual link to God is pure wisdom."

—BILLY ARCEMENT, Leadership Expert, Professional Speaker
Baton Rouge, La.

"No one is an accident, a second thought, or even an unintended surprise. *You're Something Special* empowers you to see God's individual and undeniable purpose ahead of you, a destiny only you can fulfill."

—BILL MCCONNELL, Speaker, Author, Coach
Greeley, Colo.

"When media proliferates negative thoughts, everyone, especially young people, needs a message of hope and encouragement that God made each person special, with unique gifts and talents that can bless the world. This book unlocks the special calling on your life and helps you be all that you were made to be!"

—WILLIAM FEDERER, Author, President of Amerisearch, Inc.
Fort Myers, Fla.

"Is there a piece of you that isn't unique? There was no mistake when you came into the world because the Creator God made you, and He doesn't make mistakes! Everything you are reflects this good God, so accept that, saddle up, and glorify Him with your life. Thank you, Dr. Ross and Carol Hall, for an inspirational and positive message."

—CASEY SCHROEDER, Pastor
Wheatland, Wyo.

"A delightfully crafted, faith-based book dedicated to grandchildren who seek answers to life's basic questions: Who am I, and what is my purpose? A set of questions at the end of each chapter keeps the reader on a path to self-discovery."

—BILL LAMPERES, Educator, Author
Fort Collins, Colo.

"Such a timely publication for the world we live in. I love the mix of research, analogies, and stories that deliver messages of courage, creativity, resilience, and faith."

—RHEID SCHLOSS, Inspirational and Motivational Speaker
Fort Collins, Colo.

"An easy read with many wonderful, scripturally-based thoughts about what special creations of God we are. As a grandparent, I appreciate the encouraging words to grandparents at the end of the book. Anyone who reads *You're Something Special* will be encouraged about their God-given uniqueness and purpose!"

—JOHN LUGINBUHL, Pastor
Gallup, N.M.

"This book is a great read and a welcome encouragement to anyone who questions what's special about them."

—LOWELL BURKUM, Professor of Music, retired,
Council Bluffs, Ia.

"A well written, easy to read book where readers discover their life is no accident, and they are truly something special."

—CLAIRE RICHARDSON, Preserving with Purpose
Loveland, Colo.

You're Something Special

RON ROSS AND CAROL HALL

For permissions or other inquiries:
RonRoss@PowerfulSeniors.com

Cover design by Carol Hall; cover image, iStock by Getty Images

Published in the United States by Powerful Seniors, LLC
Loveland, Colorado, USA

ISBN: 978-0-9620144-6-8
ISBN: 978-0-9620144-5-1 (ebook)

You're Something Special by Ron Ross & Carol Hall
is available on Amazon.com. For a quick link and more
information, visit https://YoureSomethingSpecial.com/

Special Sales:

Powerful Seniors publications are available at special quantity discounts when purchased in bulk by corporations, organizations, and special interest groups. Please inquire about custom imprints or excerpts to fit special needs: info@powerfulseniors.com..

DEDICATION

To grandchildren everywhere ...
and with boundless love
for two of God's special creations:

Amy Opal

"Amy, as your God-given gifts and talents bloom,
they reveal to you and the world around you
how very special you are!"

— Grandpa Ross

Annalina Coraline

"Anna, if ever you need a reminder
how special you are, just open this book
and consider Who created the extraordinary you."

— Grandma Karo

TABLE OF CONTENTS

PREFACE

Nobody ever told me I was special — that is until
the early 1970s, when I heard the Bill Gaither Trio sing
You're Something Special. As I listened to the original
soundtrack on the radio, my heart was touched by the
simple words, catchy tune, and sweet sound of children singing to each other (and to me). The song's
message, so simple yet profound, created in my spirit
a sense of wonder that still remains.

At the time, I was over 40 years old, married with
three school-age children. We lived in suburbia where
life was pleasant, predictable, and sometimes boring.
As the song played, I pondered, "Am I really something special? Does God truly have a plan and a purpose for my life?"

The song stuck in my mind, as good songs do. I
bought the record, played it often, and memorized
the words as I sang along. I taught myself to play it on
the piano; and now, three decades later, I often plunk
out the tune and sing with gusto, "I'm something special, I'm the only one of my kind..." As I sing, I consider the wonder of God's special purpose for my life —
and sometimes shed a tear.

In 2003 I wrote a series of weekly newspaper columns on the theme "you're something special." I was blessed to write them, and the readers loved them! When the series ended, I stored the writings in a three-ring-binder, knowing that someday I would revisit these popular essays.

Fifteen years later, I was moved to put the columns in book form. One delay after another interrupted the process of editing, typesetting, and all the other tasks that accompany self-publishing. Two years later, I thought the book was ready for print, so I showed the manuscript to my very special next-door neighbor, Carol Hall. She liked the content but politely insisted it needed further editing.

I relented. Carol went to work. She carefully read each chapter and made valuable edits; but, more importantly, she added illustrations, quotes, and relevant Scriptures. Carol spent uncounted hours of prayer, research, and editing that infused simple spiritual truths into each chapter. The last two chapters are the sole work of Carol's heart and hand. She also created the cover art and the general design of the book. Without Carol, *You're Something Special* would never read so good, mean so much, or look so nice.

This little book is a gift of love to all who ponder the big questions of life. Like the lyrics of the Gaither's song, the words of this book present a powerful and transforming message in a clear and simple way. As you hold it in your hand, we hope you will treasure its eternal message in your heart: "He had a special purpose that He wanted you to find. So He made you something special; you're the only one of your kind."

RON ROSS   CAROL HALL

YOU'RE SOMETHING SPECIAL

When Jesus sent you to us, we loved you from the start;
You were just a bit of sunshine from heaven to our hearts.
Not just another baby 'cause since the world began
There's been something very special for you in His plan...

That's why He made you special; you're the only one of your kind;
God gave you a body and a bright healthy mind.
He had a special purpose that He wanted you to find.
So He made you something special; you're the only one of your kind.

I have a little sister who's not at all like me;
She can write a lovely poem, but I can climb a tree.
My brother, too, is diff'rent with freckles on his nose –
When my questions need answers, he's the one who knows...

That's why I'm something special; I'm the only one of my kind;
God gave me a body and a bright healthy mind.
He had a special purpose that He wanted me to find,
So He made me something special; I'm the only one of my kind.

My daddy mows the backyard; my mommy makes the bed;
My brother cleans the playroom; I see the dog gets fed.
And each one needs the other to help him thro' the day,
And love must be the reason God planned it that way...

That's why He made me special; I'm the only one of my kind;
God gave me a body and a bright healthy mind.
He had a special purpose that He wanted me to find.
So He made me something special; I'm the only one of my kind.

Words by Gloria Gaither and William J. Gaither; Music by William J. Gaither
© 1974 Hanna Street Music (BMI) (adm. at CapitolCMGPublishing.com)
All rights reserved. Used by permission.

BILL ♪ GLORIA GAITHER

have blessed the world with their
beautiful gospel music for decades —
earning numerous Grammy and Dove awards.

In 2000, they were named ASCAP's
Christian Songwriters of the Century.
They were also inducted into the
Gospel Music Hall of Fame.

One sweet and simple children's song
with an unforgettable tune
is the inspiration for this book.
That song, released in 1996, is titled:

You're
Something
Special

To hear the Gaithers sing the entire song:

https://youtu.be/6p0qkb66phg

For more Gaither music:
Gaither.com

INTRODUCTION

Who is that person wearing your skin? Where have you come from, where are you going, and what are you supposed to do in the meantime?

Isn't it rather simple? After all, biologists can define you genetically, psychologists can explain you behaviorally, sociologists can assign you culturally, theologians can classify you religiously, educators can measure you intellectually, employers can utilize you profitably, judges can adjudicate you legally, bankers can rank you economically, and your parents can describe you proudly. Yet, still, you wonder who you are and why you're here.

The following chapters explore this wonderful subject of YOU! Each chapter focuses on a different aspect of YOU, what you're all about, and why you are special.

This book has one premise: You are not an accident; you are a unique creation of God, here for a purpose. In the 10,000-year history of humanity, there has never been anyone like you, and throughout the untold millenniums to come, there will never be anyone like you again. Indeed, ***You're Something Special!***

"He made you you-nique."

Max Lucado

Chapter 1

You're Specially Made

The first and most provable difference between you and everyone else on the planet is that no one is constructed like you. Your body is different from anyone who has ever lived or ever will live — different inside and out.

But what about identical twins? The truth is, they're different too. My neighbor has an identical twin sister whom she speaks of often. "Baby A" was born three minutes before "Baby B." At birth in the hospital, the twins wore little beaded bracelets with those words spelled out on the beads; that was the only way to tell them apart.

Over time, I heard several unusual twin-stories. One day my neighbor recounted a frightening tale of an accidental separation from her twin as a young child.

> *"Twin B" crashed headlong into a mirror! The sister she thought she spotted was her own reflection in the mirror.*

The twins were exploring one of those goofy house-of-mirrors at a carnival that came to town. Together since the womb, these two identicals were inseparable. They always held hands, but somehow in that house-of-mirrors, the twins got separated.

Missing her sister, "Twin B" panicked and ran down the mirrored hallway searching for her. Turning a corner, she spotted "Twin A"; and they ran at top speed toward each other. Then, suddenly, "Twin B" crashed headlong into a mirror! The sister she thought she spotted was her own reflection in the mirror.

These two are defined as mirror twins. Although they look and sound identical, they have unique differences. One is naturally right-handed; the other is a southpaw. The hair whorl on one twin's crown swirls clockwise; the other swirls counterclockwise. When one twin cut a new left-side tooth, her sister cut the same right-side tooth. A single egg split at fertilization, and the DNA is identical, but there are still differences in these twins. They're identical, yet unique.

A science called biometrics examines these physical differences within each human body. Biometrics refers to technologies that measure and analyze human body characteristics for authentication purposes — fingerprints, eye retinas and irises, voice patterns, facial patterns, and hand measurements.

Biometrics has proven no one's face looks like yours. If someone tells you, "My brother-in-law looks exactly like you," he doesn't. He may look "like" you, but he doesn't look "exactly like" you. He can't because there are many subtle differences in skin, hair, nose, eyes, and mouth that are definable and measurable. Even identical twins can't look exactly alike.

The rest of your body reveals even more differences. Your height, weight, hands, feet, and bellybutton all vary to some degree from others. You are made of precisely the same material as everyone else, and you may closely resemble another person, but you are constructed in a way that is unique to you.

Another aspect of your physical uniqueness is discernible in the sound of your voice. It is unique from all others: the length of your vocal cords, the shape of your oral cavity, the width and length of your tongue, the spacing and shape of your teeth, and the contour of your lips. Add to these physical differences, your unique ethnic and cultural make-up, and you have a voice that is only yours. Thanks to advances in biometrics, voiceprint technology is as precise as fingerprint technology and acceptable in courts of law.

Internally, you are also different from everyone else on earth. Your metabolism — the variety of chemical reactions that occur within your body that enable you to live, reproduce, grow, and respond to your environment — is uniquely yours. This distinctive body chemistry is why the medical and pharmaceutical industries put disclaimers and lengthy warning labels on their products and procedures. Sometimes it takes a volume of text to warn of all the possible side effects, because every human body is unique.

> *"You saw me before I was born … before I began to breathe."*
>
> Pslm. 139:16 TLB

You are unique from all the billions of people on earth — past, present, and future. That's because you are a special creation of God, as explained by the psalmist: *"You made all the delicate, inner parts of my body and knit them together in my mother's womb. Thank you for making me so wonderfully complex! It is amazing to think about. Your workmanship is marvelous — and how well I know it. You were there while I was being formed in utter seclusion! You saw me before I was born and scheduled each day of my life before I began to breathe. Every day was recorded in your book!"* (Pslm. 139:13–16 TLB)

From a physical point of view, you are created special. But along with the physical expressions of your absolute uniqueness, you are unique in many other ways. The next chapter discusses another specialness you have — your mind.

Think about it...

1. Think about all the members of your family; who do you resemble the most?

2. What remarkable physical characteristics run in your family?

3. How does the sound of your voice differ from your best friend?

Chapter 2

You Think Differently Than Others

No person on earth comprehends things as you do. No one constructs sentences or reacts to these words as you do. You have your own way of understanding people, places, things, words, and events.

Let me give you an example. If you hear a baby cry, your reaction might depend on whether or not you are a mother or just someone passing by. A mother will probably have a sense of urgency and concern, while a passerby might just keep walking.

Here's why: Everyone sees things from a different perspective, endows things with different meanings, and assigns different values to everyone and everything they encounter.

Let's consider these differences:

Perspective: You think differently than others because of your unique perspective. No one sees things precisely from the same point-of-view that you do. The Indian parable of the blind men and an elephant is a common example of this principle:

A group of blind men heard that a strange animal called an elephant had been brought to town, but none of them were aware of its shape and form. Out of curiosity, they said: "We must inspect and know it by touch, of which we are capable." So, they sought it out, and when they found the elephant, they groped about it. The first blind man, whose hand landed on the trunk, said: "This being is like a thick snake." For another, whose hand reached its ear, it seemed like "a kind of fan." As for another, whose hand was upon its leg, he said the elephant is "a pillar, like a tree trunk." The blind man who placed his hand upon its side said the elephant "is a wall." Another felt its tail, and described it as "a rope." The last felt its tusk, stating the elephant is that which is "hard and smooth, like a spear."

Your perspective will always be unique because you are the only person who experiences life the way you do. You sort out each thing that happens to you in your own way. Every person you meet, every tweet you tweet, every event you attend, every book you read, every sermon you hear, every challenge you face, every victory you win, every path you walk ... every elephant you touch ... is completely and uniquely yours.

Meaning: You think differently from others because you assign your unique meaning to things. In any town square in the world, the appearance of a cross (the symbol of Christianity), or a Star of David (the symbol of Judaism), or a crescent moon (the symbol of Islam) would each cause a different reaction from the individuals who view them because of the varying meanings they assign to each icon.

And consider logos. A Chevrolet logo might represent "the good ole days" and bring joy to a senior who once owned a '57 Chevy. But it could trigger grief for a MADD mom who lost her son to a drunk, driving a Corvette way too fast.

One of the most famous logos in the world is the Apple logo, but do you know what that apple with the bite in it means? You might guess "fresh," like a new way of computing; or "natural and enjoyable," like user-friendly; or "tempting," like a very desirable product. Right or wrong,

We live in a world controlled by emotion with very little intellect involved.

you will give an answer that's meaningful to you. To prove the point, Google the question and you'll get an assortment of answers.

Values: You think differently because of your personal values. What you see or experience becomes good or bad, right or wrong, important or unimportant, repulsive or attractive, dangerous or safe, humorous or distasteful, etc. based on your values. Your values flow from your morals, religion, customs, ethnicity, social class, etc. — all blended in a way unique to you. Typically, your values serve as your moral compass.

Does this mean you have your truth, and I have my truth? Certainly not! You can believe the earth is flat or Elvis is still alive, but that doesn't make it true. Even seeing something doesn't make it true. Ask any three eyewitnesses to a car accident to tell you what happened, and each of their stories will differ to some degree, yet there is only one accurate narrative of the event. Einstein nailed it when he said, "The world as we have created it is a process of our thinking. It cannot be changed without changing our thinking."

Some people equate thinking with feeling, as if they're interchangeable. You can "feel" that something is real, but feelings don't authenticate anything except feelings. Unfortunately, emotional feelings often impede rational thinking and trigger inappropriate and regrettable actions. It's easy and foolish to act on your emotions without first consulting your brain.

Thomas Edison noted, "Five percent of the people think; ten percent of the people think they think; and the other eighty-five percent would rather die than think." If Edison's observation is anywhere near correct, we live in a world controlled by emotion with very little intellect involved.

Your thoughts are all yours. You own them, so you can choose what to think; however, the Bible warns, *"Be careful how you think; your life is shaped by your thoughts."* (Prov. 4:23 GNT) The way you discern things is also unique to you, so it's best to test your judgment with objective facts, compare meanings and values with reality, and keep an open mind to the possibility of misperception. It's important to remember the human tendency is to see things your way.

In times of hardship or trouble, your thoughts are especially critical, and negative thinking can only darken your life. Jonah found himself in a whale of trouble, yet he turned to God and was saved: *"When I had lost all hope, I turned my thoughts once more to the Lord"* (Jonah 2:7 TLB). When life feels hopeless, don't fall into a pattern of negative thinking. Instead, think about the goodness of God; know that His light and His purpose in your life are greater than any darkness.

Your thoughts control your emotions and your life, and God gave you authority over your thoughts; so guard carefully what you think: *"Finally, brothers, whatever is true, whatever is honorable, whatever is just, whatever is pure, whatever is lovely, whatever is commendable, if there is any excellence, if there is anything worthy of praise, think about these things."* (Phil. 4:8 ESV)

Think about it…

1. Think about the story of the blind men and the elephant. How can they all be right about what they personally experience and yet be wrong about their description of an elephant?

2. Is there something you see often, such as a statue, building, logo, etc., that has special meaning to you?

3. How do you decide what is right and what is wrong?

*"Let's not forget
that the little emotions
are the great captains of our lives
and we obey them without realizing it."*

Vincent van Gogh

Chapter 3

You Have a Distinctive Way of Feeling

What you hate, love, fear, laugh at, cry about, or passively observe is determined by your own unique and wholly-owned emotional structure. You and I could cheer for the same football team, yet experience the game differently. You could attend a concert with your best friend, and a different song would move each of you. Two girlfriends for life could watch the same sad movie, and one would cry while the other would not.

Varied responses to the same event occur because each of us places a different emotional value on every word spoken, every deed performed, and every event observed. To add to the conundrum, your emotions aren't always consistent; what excites you on Monday may bore you on Thursday. "A feeling is no longer the same when it comes the second time. It dies through awareness of its return. We become tired and weary of our feelings when they come too often and last too long." (Pascal Mercier)

Emotions are how you respond to a feeling of pain, pleasure, attraction, repulsion, etc. They are physiological responses linked to thoughts — and are as unique to you as your DNA.

Think about it; can you remember the last time you felt something so deeply you wept? Can you remember the last time you were truly afraid, filled with joy, or consumed with anger? Have you ever felt the need to apologize for your emotional response?

If you can control your thoughts, you can tame your emotions.

It's true for everyone, unless you're a total stoic, sometimes your emotions get the upper hand. But that doesn't mean you're a slave to your emotions and have no control over them. Quite the contrary: Emotions are slaves to your thoughts. And, although it's easier said than done, if you can control your thoughts, you can tame your emotions. Oscar Wilde realized this when he said, "I don't want to be at the mercy of my emotions. I want to use them and to dominate them."

Nothing influences every aspect of your life as much as your emotions. Your emotions are the arbiter of the extremes between passion and indifference, love and hate, faith and fear, hope and despair, joy and sorrow, pleasure and irritation, or anger and calm.

Do you remember how you felt when you bought a new car? Do you remember your feelings when you saw the first dent or scratch on that car? How about the first time a girlfriend or boyfriend dumped you? Did you ever lose a job, or win a championship, or fall down in public, or earn a degree, or give birth to a child, or bury a mate, or laugh until you cried, or cry until you laughed, or jump for joy, or weep for hours? Of course, you have.

The point is, your emotions impact everything in your life. They empower you or emasculate you, clarify your thoughts or confuse them, embarrass you or appease you, scare you or comfort you. How well you understand and manage your feelings is one of life's greatest challenges because any change in your world will fuel your kettle of emotions to some degree.

It's wonderful to jump for joy, laugh 'til you cry, or fall madly in love; God wants that for you. But negative emotions — like anger, jealousy, or bitterness — are often the ones that boil over and take control, especially right after they've been triggered. The Bible warns: *"A man without self-control is like a city broken into and left without walls."* (Prov. 25:28 ESV) Next time you feel your emotions boiling over, think of that analogy. Allowing negative emotions to simmer indefinitely is also detrimental, as negative feelings can become inbred and surface far too frequently. That's why forgiveness is essential.

Your emotions are real, however, and it's important you do not deny or vilify them but rather try to understand and live in mindful-harmony with your feelings. Thank God for the ability to feel emotion. It's one of His perpetual gifts to you — a gift to steward wisely and use for Him.

Someone once said if you use a dictionary to complete the sentence, "I feel _____," you could list almost 2000 words. That's a lot of emotion to experience! The way you deal with those emotions is very much a part of what makes you something special.

Think about it...

1. Think about something that makes you sad, then something that makes you happy.

2. Who is the funniest person you know? What makes them funny?

3. How well do you manage your emotions, especially the negative ones like anger, fear, frustration, etc.?

*"I know He made me special
and with a purpose."*

Ainsley Earhardt

Chapter 4

You're Here For a Reason

You are no accident. You're not the descendant of an ape, nor will you one day return to earth as a bunny rabbit, a Billy goat, or a British Lord or Lady. You're here at a specific time, living in a particular place, with an important mission to accomplish. Your life has meaning — you are here for a reason.

You know this is true. Deep inside the depths of your soul, you sense an eternal-ness, an awareness of destiny, a feeling that you are someone unique in the 10,000-year history of humankind.

You're right, and modern science agrees with you. With the discovery of the complexity of DNA, scientists consistently give testimony in court declaring an individual's DNA is unequivocal evidence of that person's unique identity.

But, if you and I are unique and special, why is it that we do so little to fulfill our destiny? Two reasons:

First, significance comes to those who seek it. Most people don't find meaning in life because they let life happen to them rather than make something meaningful out of each day, week, or month. They live as spectators rather than participants, victims rather than victors. Blind and deaf from age two, Helen Keller didn't have the choice to live as a spectator. Her victorious spirit led her to write, "The only thing worse than being blind is having sight but no vision."

Second, to fulfill your destiny requires an open mind and a big heart. Many people live a small, self-centered life, striving only to satisfy their wants and needs. Others want to be served rather than serve, so they become takers rather than givers, which can evolve into a sense of entitlement.

A narrow, inward perspective such as this fosters greed and scarcity rather than generosity and abundance, which is not conducive to discovering or fulfilling one's destiny. Jesus teaches the value of giving: *"Give, and you will receive. Your gift will return to you in full — pressed down, shaken together to make room for more, running over, and poured into your lap. The amount you give will determine the amount you get back."* (Luke 6:38 NLT)

Often, people think of money when they hear the word "give," but Jesus isn't referring to just monetary gifts. There are endless pathways for giving (time, love, skills, companionship, assistance, knowledge, etc.), and each holds potential for discovery, opportunity, and growth.

God created you special for a reason. Ask Him to guide you as you seek to discover your purpose. He will answer you. Jesus says, *"Keep on asking, and you will receive what you ask for. Keep on seeking, and you will find. Keep on knocking, and the door will be opened for you."* (Matt. 7:7 NLT)

Start today. Demand answers to life's two greatest questions: "Who am I?" and "Why am I here?" Your answers to those questions are found deep within your soul and in quiet, persistent reflection.

Discovering your purpose is a very individual task worthy of every thought, prayer, and effort you can give. Helen Keller also noted, "What I am looking for is not out there, it is in me."

Start by looking inside. Take note of what you love; what you feel passionate about; what makes you cry, or laugh, or frown; what you do well; what makes you happy; what problems you solve, what needs you meet, what hurts you heal. When you find the answers, you begin to understand the reason you are here and why you are so special.

Think about it...

1. Have you ever asked yourself the question: Who am I? What's your answer?

2. What do you like to do that makes you feel good about yourself and others?

3. You are here for a purpose. What has God placed on your heart that you feel passionate about?

*"A winner is someone
who recognizes his God-given talents,
works his tail off to develop them into skills,
and uses these skills to accomplish his goals."*

Larry Bird

Chapter 5

You Have Unique Gifts and Talents

The specific combination of natural gifts and talents you have is unique to you. No one on earth has had or ever will have the same mix of abilities, interests, and passions. This mix is part of what makes you unique — something special.

It would be helpful if, at birth, you came with a spec sheet stating what God designed you to do.

Too many people go through life without taking a close look at the gifts and talents they possess, and so they live a less fulfilling life. But it's never too late to live life at a much more meaningful level. However, you must discover, develop, and use the special gifts and talents God has given you, remembering, *"Every good gift and every perfect gift is from above..."* (James 1:17 KJV)

Discovering your natural gifts and talents is an enlightening **adventure**. It would be helpful if, at birth, you came with a spec sheet stating what God designed you to do. Though the Bible is full of instructions for humanity, God didn't include custom, individual specifications; therefore, you must go on your personal "gifts and talents discovery tour."

Your tour begins early in life as you explore the variety of possibilities: You try this and experiment with that; you find out what is easy and what is difficult; you learn what you feel passionate about and what you don't.

This discovery is very important; it's why your parents made you take piano lessons or dance classes, or why they pushed you to join a softball league or swim team. They wanted you to try a variety of things, to uncover your interests and talents. But the discovery tour doesn't end with graduation from high school or college, or with retirement. It goes on for a lifetime because, as you age, the things you can and cannot do and the things that interest you will change.

Discovering your gifts and talents is an adventure; developing them is a priority; using them is a joy.

Once you discover some of your unique gifts and talents, you must make it a **priority** to develop them into skills. The most naturally talented musicians take music lessons and practice conscientiously, and the most gifted athletes still need coaches. Tiger Woods, one of the greatest golfers in history, had several coaches. If Tiger needs help to develop his skills, do you suppose you too might need some help?

Discovering and developing your gifts and talents is a life-long process, stimulated by an endless world of provocative opportunities and events. For instance, after the tragedy of September 11, 2001, at the age of 80, my father became curious about the teachings of Islam. So he researched and wrote a comparative analysis of Islam and Christianity.

Discovering your gifts and talents is an **adventure**; developing them is a **priority**; using them is a **joy.** But, the prerequisite to using your gifts and talents correctly is to understand that God intends you to use them within the context of a moral and virtuous life.

According to His plan — which is always what's best for you — God infuses pleasure as you do things at which you are gifted. It doesn't feel as much like "work" when you work with your natural talents on something you have great passion for and possess excellent skills to accomplish. Working "with" your gifts and talents helps ensure success, and can transform a task from work into pleasure.

You yearn to live a life with meaning and purpose — a life where usefulness and service define your mission, and joy is your reward. That's exactly what happens when your gifts, talents, and work align with God's unique design and special desire for your life.

Think about it...

1. What are you naturally good at doing?

2. How can you improve at what you already do quite well?

3. How can you best use your gifts and talents?

*"You are most like your Creator
when you're being creative."*

Rick Warren

Chapter 6

You're Born Creative

Artists and musicians are not the sole proprietors of creativity. You too are creative.

Remember when you were a child, and you could fly airplanes, drive trucks, dress like a princess, or travel around the world, all within the confines of your living room? What happened to that imagination, to those uninhibited crea-tive forces? Where has the sense of adventure gone?

"The creative adult is the child who survived."

Ursula Leguin

In 1968, a research study was conducted on 1,600 children ages 3–5 years old using the George Land

Creativity Test. The children were retested at 10 and 15 years of age. The results are astounding:

Age 5:   Average creativity score = 98%
Age 10: Average creativity score = 30%
Age 15: Average creativity score = 12%
Adult: Average creativity score = 2%
         (280,000 adults tested)

This test concludes we are born highly creative; however, non-creative behavior is learned rapidly. In just five years, the average creativity score plummets from 98% at age 5 to 30% at age 10. And it doesn't stop there: adults score a pitiful 2% on creativity. Novelist Ursula Le Guin accurately noted, "The creative adult is the child who survived."

Each of us is born with an abundance of creativity. This should come as no surprise since God, the Creator of the entire universe, made us in His image: *"So God created mankind in his own image, in the image of God he created them; male and female he created them."* (Gen. 1:27 NIV) Unlike any other creature, as an image-bearer of God, humans possess the ability to create and to delight in that creation.

God designed you with a unique mix of gifts and talents, along with a superabundance of creativity — a

God-like quality you share with Him. But early in life, you may have been taught to stay within the lines of your coloring book, or scolded for creating mud pies on the barbecue grill. It's possible music was rare, dance was absent, stories were missing, or playmates were scarce. Such creativity-crushing scenarios are all too common.

It's easy to see how loss of creativity starts early in life, fading fast like a muscle that atrophies from lack of exercise. As you use your creativity, it grows and becomes more natural. Sadly, in formative years much potential goes unnoticed, unnurtured, undeveloped — even discouraged — while creativity withers. Like any muscle, you use it or lose it.

Fortunately, there are many ways to arouse and strengthen your creativity. Here are a few:

Enjoy performing arts. As a spectator or a performer, the real-time experience of theatre, music, dance, etc. stirs your emotions and ignites your creativity. The acrobatics of Cirque du Soleil; the grace of Swan Lake Ballet; and the bands, choirs, and performing arts in your home town all kindle creativity.

Look at beautiful things. As with anything of beauty, masterpieces inspire us and enhance our creativity. I remember when I saw Michelangelo's magnificent Pieta in St. Peter's Basilica. I get chills just writing about it, and that was 40 years ago. However, you don't have to go to Rome to enjoy the beauty of a tiny flower or the majesty of a sunset. In museums and in nature, visual art is everywhere.

Travel. On our honeymoon, my wife and I wandered the side roads of Wyoming, and for over 50 years we never stopped wandering. Our travels took us around the world — to over 20 countries, and to all but three states. But sightseeing can easily be a local experience. Go somewhere near yet off your beaten path and discover something new to excite your senses and trigger your creativity.

Encourage your dreams. "You're either dreaming, or you're dying."(Rick Warren) But how can you dream without making time for it? Take a stroll and let your mind wander, or spend time dreaming out the window each day. You coddle your creativity as you encourage and explore your dreams. This happens naturally because you inherently know, "Man alone, has the power transform his thoughts into physical reality; man, alone, can dream and make his dreams come true." (Napoleon Hill)

Look with the eyes of a child. Remember the magic of youth: your sense of wonder, love of color, spontaneous movement, curiosity with everything, and urge to explore. Remember when life was fascinating. For awhile each day, look through those childhood eyes and recall your childhood imagination. Be curious, and you will arouse your dormant creativity.

"We are God's handiwork, created in Christ Jesus to do good works, which God prepared in advance for us to do." (Eph. 2:10 NIV) You were created for a purpose, and God designed you with the unique mix of gifts and talents necessary to accomplish that purpose. Along with those gifts and talents, He shared His creativity with you — more than enough creativity to give life to your purpose and purpose to your life.

"God made you to be creative." (Rick Warren)

Think about it...

1. What is the most beautiful thing you have ever seen?

2. Who is the most interesting person you have ever met? What makes them interesting?

3. If you could ask God one question, what would that question be?

"Creativity is intelligence having fun."

Albert Einstein

*"It takes courage to show up
and become who you really are."*

e.e. cummings

Chapter 7

You Have Hidden Courage

There is a large variety of spiders in Africa, some poisonous, and all quite scary. One weekend my wife Amy had a close encounter with one of those large spiders, which was at least the size of a saucer!

She was home alone with our two toddler children in a tiny house located about 11 miles into the bush from Lusaka, Zambia. Amy was more than alone, as I was out of town, and she had no vehicle, no telephone, and no electricity. She was about a quarter of a mile from the nearest neighbor, with no streetlights and no paved roads. In the late afternoon, Amy noticed a large spider dashing between the rafters of our unfinished cement-block house, which had a roof but no ceiling. As daylight quickly vanished, she tried to reach the spider to kill it, but it hid in the shadows between the rafters and the roof.

After sunset Amy lit a candle, prepared our two children for bed, and read them several bedtime stories. All the while, she kept to herself the fear she felt for her unwelcome guest hiding in the rafters.

> *"Courage is fear that has said its prayers."*
>
> Dorothy Bernard

She tucked the children in bed and then moved cautiously through the shadows of the house into our bedroom. Before going to bed, she took one more peek into the children's room and found them safe and asleep. Relieved, she returned to the bedroom and put her candle on the small bedside table.

Before blowing out the candle, Amy glanced nervously around the dimly lit room and breathed a silent prayer for the rapid arrival of two things: courage and daylight. She knew there was a large and potentially deadly spider somewhere in her house, and there was nothing she could do to find it or kill it or chase it away. So she blew out her candle, laid her head down on the pillow, and soon, in the remote darkness of the African night, she went to sleep. That's courage.

The Bible confirms, *"For God gave us a spirit not of fear but of power and love and self-control."* (2 Tim. 1:7 ESVUK). These are the virtues that got a nervous mother, alone with two small children, through the blackest night of her life. Amy personified courage as she prayerfully closed her eyes. Deep within, her spirit instinctively knew what it would take to fall asleep: "Courage is fear that has said its prayers." (Dorothy Bernard)

> *"Fear calls us to be spectators. Courage calls us to get in the game."*
>
> Dave Cornell

You do not know what kind of courage you have deep within your soul until you face a situation that calls it forth. Most of us have far more courage than we realize. Sure, you've probably seen yourself fail the courage test from time to time. You kept silent when you should have spoken up; you succumbed to peer pressure when you should have walked away; perhaps you ran and hid when you should have stood and fought.

"Fear calls us to be spectators. Courage calls us to get in the game." (Dave Cornell)

But don't let your present fears or past failures determine the level of courage you are capable of displaying. Remember God's reassuring words: *"Be strong and courageous. Do not be frightened, and do not be dismayed, for the Lord your God is with you wherever you go."* (Josh. 1:9 ESVU)

Helen Keller affirmed this scripture prior to her 40,000 mile journey around the world at age 74. Blind, deaf, and unafraid, before boarding the airplane she typed this message to inquiring journalists: "It is wonderful to climb the liquid mountains of the sky. Behind me and before me is God, and I have no fears."

"... liquid mountains of the sky"— such a beautiful description of clouds could not have come from a fearful soul.

You're something special. God gave you his Holy Spirit — a spirit of power, love, and self-control — so you too can face with courage the saucer-sized spiders of daily life.

Think about it...

1. What scares you most?

2. Think about a time when you were afraid but were courageous. How did you feel when it was all over, and you were safe?

3. Go to Dictionary.com and look up the word "courageous." Does it describe you?

*"Faith is not belief without proof,
but trust without reservation."*

D. Elton Trueblood

Chapter 8

You Can Live With Faith

The various definitions of faith and the true meaning of faith do not always correspond. Wikipedia's explanation of faith begins with this line: "Faith is belief in an idea that is unsupported or contradicted by evidence ... largely reserved for concepts of religion."

Like a WIFI connection, faith is invisible; but you know it has the power to connect you to what you need.

"Unsupported or contradicted by evidence"... Humbug! That's not faith; that's stupidity.

Faith is not something for weak minds or emotional morons. True faith engages the mind, the emotions, and the will for a confident anticipation of advantage. Like a WIFI connection, faith is invisible; but you know it has the power to connect you to what you need.

> *Faith without some foundation is fantasy.*

First of all, for there to be real faith, **the mind must be engaged.** Real faith is founded on facts first. Blind faith (what Wikipedia's naïve writers describe) is not concerned with reality, facts, or truth.

Blind faith says, "I've made up my mind; don't confuse me with the facts." Real faith wants the facts, seeks the truth, and advances from there. Faith without some foundation is fantasy.

Physicist Albert Einstein was a self-proclaimed agnostic; yet quotes reveal his work involved an element of faith he deemed essential — a faith based on the laws of nature. Near the end of his life, Einstein said, "If you ask me to prove what I believe, I can't ... The mind can proceed only so far upon what it knows and can prove. There comes a point where the mind takes a leap ... and comes out upon a higher plane of knowledge, but can never prove how it got there. All great discoveries have involved such a leap."

Adopting the same word, "leap," Christian evangelist Billy Graham explained, "No matter how much knowledge you gather, no matter how much proof you accumulate, you will never know the Lord Jesus Christ without taking the certain leap of faith that salvation comes only from Him."

Billy Graham and Albert Einstein appear to agree: although it involves a leap, faith is grounded in facts and truth — both in the spiritual realm of religion and the secular field of science.

Next, for there to be real faith, **the emotions must be involved.** There is no faith without hope, and hope sustains positive emotions. The Bible defines faith as "... *confidence in what we hope for and assurance about what we do not see."* (Heb. 11:1 NIV)

For two people to agree to be joined together in marriage is an act of faith that requires significant hope, combined with emotional devotion to persevere through good times and bad, health and sickness. Similarly, for an entrepreneur to take his or her life savings and risk it on a business venture requires a belief in the viability of his business plan and his skills, despite the lack of a solid guarantee of profit.

To rely solely on emotions for decisions related to religion, relationships, business, or life in general, is to surrender logic or truth to the whims of sensation. On the other hand, to deny that emotions contribute to life is to live without hope and die without love.

And finally, for there to be real faith, **the will must be involved.** You can know something (mind), and you can feel something (emotion), but unless you do something (action), what you know and what you feel will slowly fade. Many people, afraid to act on what they know and feel, live lives of bitterness and regret. They spend their days wondering what would have happened if only they had _____. (Fill in the blank)

Faith exists when what you know and what you feel gives you the confidence to move bravely forward. Faith is crucial in getting through the trials of life; in living a life of peace, hope and joy; and in discovering your purpose in life.

Two roads lead into tomorrow: the road of doubt and despair, and the road of faith and hope. Blessings will enrich your journey when your mind, your heart and your will, in grand agreement, take an educated, calculated, optimistic risk — a leap of faith — and travel down the hopeful road.

Think about it...

1. Describe the difference between blind faith and real faith?

2. Why must real faith involve your will?

3. Name one or two areas of your life where your faith is strong. What areas are weak?

"That the birds of worry and care fly over your head, this you cannot change; but that they build nests in your hair, this you can prevent."

Chinese Proverb

Chapter 9

You Don't Have to Worry

Each of these three scenarios is an occasion for worry:

(1) Don, a recent college grad from Wyoming was offered a job in the hub of New York City. His parents are concerned about his transition from rural to urban life. (2) A businessman watched carefully as a competitor opened a business two blocks away. (3) Grandmother scheduled her yearly physical and is apprehensive about what may be found.

Don's parents could spend time and energy conjuring up all the bad things that might happen as their small-town son exchanges the peace of Wyoming for the chaos of New York City. The worrisome possibilities are endless.

A businessman could sit and stew about how the competition will cause him to lose his business, which will cause him to lose his house, which will possibly lead to a divorce. Meanwhile, he won't have any time to think about the positive things he could do right now to solidify his customer base, expand his product lines, revitalize his marketing, etc.

You must deny worry a resting place in your soul.

A grandmother in her mid-70s imagines all the things that could be wrong with her. She probably heard the latest information about the many risks and consequences of a stroke, and now what if it happens to her? She could worry herself into an avalanche of ailments.

These are examples of destructive, negative self-talk that distract the mind from solving the real problems at hand. Excessive worry can ignite the imagination, and often in detrimental ways. "If you treat every situation as a life and death matter, you'll die a lot of times." (Dean Smith)

You must take those negative worrisome thoughts that enter your mind and change them into creative ideas that result in positive solutions. You must deny worry a resting place in your soul because a byproduct of worry is fear; God did not give you a spirit of fear. "There is a great difference between worry and concern. A worried person sees a problem, and a concerned person solves a problem." (Harold Stephen)

What's important is what you can do today about the problems you face today. Yesterday is gone, and tomorrow's not yet here. Today is what you have to deal with, and worry doesn't get anything done. *"Therefore do not worry about tomorrow, for tomorrow will worry about itself. Each day has enough trouble of its own."* (Jesus, Matt. 6:34 NIV)

And when you've done all you can do to solve a problem, trust your decisions and take your stand. Stop overthinking. Things will happen as they happen. Don't worry about what you cannot change.

"If your problem has a solution, why worry about it? If your problem doesn't have a solution, why worry about it?" (Chinese proverb)

Think about it…

1. What do you worry about most?

2. Think about a time you worried about something, and then everything worked out.

3. How do you deal with the unknown events of the future?

"Sorrow looks back,
worry looks around,
faith looks up."

Ralph Waldo Emerson

"I failed my way to success."

Thomas Edison

Chapter 10

You Can Define Success

What is your definition of success?

The dictionary defines success as "a favorable or de-
sired outcome; the attainment of wealth, favor, or em-
inence." However, this definition is short-sighted and
inadequate. Based on Webster's definition, the possible meanings of success are endless, for example:

If you're broke, success means wealth.
If you're sick, success means health.
If you're lonely, success means friendship.
If you're homeless, success means a place to live.
If you're lost, success means being found.
If you're disorganized, success means order.
If you're unloved, success means romance.
If you're unknown, success means fame.
If you're infamous, success means anonymity.

If you're in prison, success means freedom.
If you're in debt, success means "paid in full."
If you're in doubt, success means confidence.
If you're fearful, success means faith.
If you're uneducated, success means knowledge.
If you're sad, success means joy.
If you're always in a hurry, success means patience.
If you're weary, success means vitality.
If you're abrasive, success means gentleness.
If you're prideful, success means humility.
If you're callous, success means compassion.
If you're undisciplined, success means self-control.
If you're on the outside, success means inclusion.

As time passes, your definition of success will change because, all too often, it is defined by whatever you want most right now; success equates to getting your immediate desires met. What you need or want this very moment is what attracts your attention, expends your energy, picks your pocket, consumes your time, and may affect your future.

It's not the money or status that's the problem; it's the love of those things.

This near-sighted success often targets wealth, power, or fame. Such myopic success is fickle, and fulfillment is ofttimes fleeting. It's not the money or status that's the problem; it's the love of those things. Solomon described it this way: *"But as I looked at everything I had worked so hard to accomplish, it was all so meaningless — like chasing the wind ..."* (Eccl. 2:11 NLT)

If you ask a Christian who is the most successful person ever to live, a likely response would be, "Jesus Christ." But Jesus was homeless and penniless, a convicted criminal, brutally beaten and crucified. Such a life doesn't seem to equate with Webster's definition of success; yet before He died, Jesus said three words

> *Success is finishing what God has called you to do.*

that defined true success. He said, *"It is finished."* Jesus knew he had fulfilled his purpose on earth.

Success is finishing what God has called you to do.

Jesus had a purpose in life, and so do you. You were in the womb only nine months, but God had all eternity to plan your life. He designed you for a purpose,

He loves you, and He wants you to be successful. *"For we are God's handiwork created in Christ Jesus to do good works, which God prepared in advance for us to do."* (Eph. 2:10 NIV)

God gave you all the tools needed for your success. He made you something special, so you can succeed at what He's calling you to do. Rather than chase the wind, discover God's purpose for your life. Then you can define success.

Think about it ...

1. Review the list at the beginning of this chapter and mark two or three items that mean success to you.

2. What God-given tools (gifts, talents, passions, personality) can you employ to be successful?

3. Who is the most successful person you know? What do you think makes that person successful?

*"Life without problems
is a school without lessons."*

Anonymous

Chapter 11

You Can Solve Problems

"I suppose you think your problems are worse than mine, right? Well, let me tell you something, pal — you don't know anything about having problems until you've taken a look at MY troubles!"

Is that how you feel about your problems? Do you think no one else has ever faced what you face? Does it look like your problems are enormous, but others' are insignificant?

Below are five universal truths about problems:

Universal truth #1: **Everyone has problems**. My counseling professor at Creighton University, Robert McEniry, MA, Ph.D., S.J., told our class you could walk up to anyone on the street and say in an empathetic tone, "I heard about your problem." He explained,

"Though you wouldn't know what their problem was, they would know — because everyone has problems."

Universal truth #2: **You'll always have problems.** Both rich and poor people have money problems. Married and single people have relationship troubles. Men and women have gender issues. Teenagers and old-agers have aging problems. No matter who you are or where you live, or how much you have or don't have, one thing you will always have is problems. Jesus says, *"In this world you will have trouble. But take heart! I have overcome the world."* (John 16:33 NIV)

> *Problems serve a purpose in your life.*

Universal truth #3: **Problems serve a purpose.** The apostle Paul teaches, *"We continue to shout our praise even when we're hemmed in with troubles, because we know how troubles can develop passionate patience in us, and how that patience in turn forges the tempered steel of virtue, keeping us alert for whatever God will do next."* (Rom. 5:3-4 Msg)

A problem-free life does not make life more meaningful or strengthen your patience and endurance, but facing problems does. Every problem you face is a lesson, an opportunity for learning and growth.

Universal truth #4: **Most problems can be solved — or survived.** Remember your middle school math class and those pesky multiplication and division problems your teacher gave you? For some students — especially left-brainers like me — those were difficult challenges that required intense focus to find a solution, but they all had an answer. It didn't seem like it at the time, but those math problems were good training for life. Not only did I learn most problems are solvable, but I also learned the value of endurance: If I could hang in and survive middle school math, I could probably make it through anything.

Universal truth #5: **People good at solving problems have a solution-oriented mindset, not a problem-oriented mindset.** People who see challenges as opportunities and who live their lives as victors are much better at solving problems than those with a negative attitude and a victim mentality.

Even though the problems you face may be huge, complicated, and even life-threatening, believe you can resolve them. The solutions to your troubles may call forth the very best you have and demand great courage, faith, and endurance. If so, remind yourself that you are something special, created in the image of God; and problems serve a purpose in your life.

Here's how God wants you to face life's problems as they inevitably come your way:

1. **Learn all the facts:** *"What a shame. Yes, how stupid to decide before knowing the facts!"* (Prov. 18:13 TLB)

2. **Be open to new ideas:** *"The intelligent man is always open to new ideas. In fact, he looks for them."* (Prov. 18:15 TLB)

3. **Listen to both sides of the story:** *"Any story sounds true until someone tells the other side and sets the record straight."* (Prov. 18:17 TLB)

4. **Know that God's purpose for your life is good, despite your immediate problems:** *"And we know that in all things God works for the good of those who love Him, who have been called according to His purpose."* (Rom. 8:28 NIV)

5. **Realize problems are an opportunity for growth:** *"Consider it pure joy, my brothers, whenever you face trials of many kinds, because you know that the testing of faith develops perseverance. Let perseverance finish its work so that you may be mature and complete, not lacking anything."* (James 1: 2-4 NIV)

6. **Ask God to help solve your problems:** *"If you want to know what God wants you to do, ask Him, and He will gladly tell you, for He is always ready to give a bountiful supply of wisdom to all who ask Him; He will not resent it."* (James 1:5 TLB) "Wisdom" here means good judgment — exactly what you need to solve problems.

7. **Trust God for guidance:** *"If you want favor with both God and man, a reputation for good judgment and common sense, then trust the Lord completely; don't ever trust yourself. In everything you do, put God first, and He will direct you and crown your efforts with success."* (Prov. 3:4-6 TLB)

Think about it...

1. Think about a big problem you had that you were able to solve. What lesson did you learn?

2. How do you usually act or react when you suddenly face a dilemma?

3. Would you say you have a solution-oriented mindset or a problem-oriented mindset?

Chapter 12

You Can Overcome Obstacles

Accomplishment is about overcoming obstacles.

If you want to become a brain surgeon, river-raft the Amazon, or become a world-class salesperson, you'll have to find your way around, over, or through a minefield of obstacles. The size of that minefield is in direct proportion to the size of your objective. Set big goals, and you'll face some huge challenges; attempt nothing significant, and little will stand in your way.

Here is one simple suggestion for overcoming the obstacles that discourage you from achieving your goals: **take one step forward.** No big leap, no jump to the top, no blind swan dive off the cliff; just take one step forward. I give this advice for three reasons:

The first reason is that **one step is all you can take at a time.** When I decided to get a post-graduate degree, I had a wife, three children, a full-time job, and no tuition. So I took one class — that's all — just one class. A few years later, I earned my Master's Degree.

The second reason to take one step forward is that, in many cases, **one step will cause your obstacle to flee** like a scared rabbit. Many of the barriers you see in front of you appear larger than they are. Face them, step into them, confront them with even the smallest step forward, and you will notice they are not the imposing monsters you once thought.

The third reason to take a step forward is that, over time, **an accumulation of small steps grants you victory.** Your determination will break down barriers, and your endurance will power you through obstacles. Albert Einstein recognized this when he admitted, "I know quite certainly that I myself have no special talent; curiosity, obsession and dogged endurance ... have brought me to my ideas."

> *... one step will cause your obstacle to flee like a scared rabbit.*

The Bible abounds with lessons on endurance: *"Slowly, steadily, surely, the time approaches when the vision will be fulfilled. If it seems slow, wait patiently, for it will surely take place. It will not be delayed."* (Hab. 2:3 NLT) Patiently persevere as you overcome obstacles — one by one.

But do you know the biggest obstacle you will face each day? It is not the mountain in the path before you; it is the monster of fear inside you. You are the biggest obstacle you face. There will always be more reasons to quit than persevere, to forfeit than fight, or to hesitate rather than take another step forward.

A friend of mine climbed Mt. Kilimanjaro in Africa. He told me, "The closer we got to the top, the more difficult it became. We were short of air, exhausted from the climb, but so close to the summit. During the last few yards to the top, all we thought about was putting one foot in front of the other."

That's what you must do in the presence of obstacles: choose your path wisely, take one step forward — and then another. Persevere, and remind yourself, *"I can do all things through him who strengthens me."* (Phil. 4:13 ESV)

History remembers and celebrates those who persevere but forgets those who give up. God designed you to persist; He made you to endure. You were created to conquer obstacles and accomplish much; you're something special.

Think about it...

1. Why is fear a common emotion associated with obstacles? What about anger?

2. When faced with an obstacle, why is it wise to take small steps forward into the barrier until you overcome?

3. What obstacle stands between you and your goals? What small step can you take to overcome that obstacle?

*"The good thing is I picked a profession
I'm passionate about."*

Ainsley Earhardt

Chapter 13

You Have God-Given Passion

You've had lots of different goals, right? You wrote them down, posted them on your refrigerator, read them every morning, dreamed about them during the night, and worked on them during the day. Some of your goals were known only to you — secreted in your heart.

It's not only the goals you set but also the passions you own that lead you to achieve.

If you were honest, you would have to admit you have not reached most of your goals. And if you were really honest, you would have to admit you didn't achieve them because they weren't that important. But you are successful in some areas. Many of your achievements in life were likely accomplished without even thinking about them as goals. You did them because you wanted to.

Let me say it again, "you did them because you wanted to." That's quite a statement, isn't it? In the final analysis, it's not only the goals you set but also the passions you own that lead you to achieve — because passion generates endurance; endurance leads to achievement; and achievement, in turn, increases passion.

... it's your internal, God-given passions that drive you.

Achievement, you see, demands much, including extra effort. No one goes the extra mile, works overtime, practices another hour, ignores defeat, disregards discouraging reports, learns another skill, alters the way they do business, or changes their behavior — unless they really want to. That's passion.

External goals may guide you, vision boards may challenge you, affirmations may remind you, but it's your internal, God-given passions that drive you. Think about this: When you pursue your passions, hardly anything can stop you. You may fall many times; you may face obstacles that delay your progress; and you may work long, hard, and all alone. But if you are pursuing your passions, you are doing what you want to do, what you believe in; therefore, you have little need for external motivation.

The question isn't only, "What are your goals?" Consider also, "What are your passions?" Goals are a target, a bull's eye at which to shoot your arrow; but passions are what send the quiver flying. They compel you to begin, sustain you in suffering, nourish you in weakness, and smile on you in achievement. They are a constant source of energy: "Passion is energy. Feel the power that comes from focusing on what excites you." (Oprah Winfrey)

Jeremiah described his passion as *"... a fire that burns in my bones and I can't hold it in ..."* (Jer. 1:9 TLB) When Jeremiah used this "fire in my bones" metaphor, he described the compelling power of passion; however, passion doesn't live in your bones. It lives in your heart. It's a product of all the unique interests, affections, hopes, and dreams that God instilled in your heart when he created you. It's a Divine spark.

Zeal, energy, spark, fire — they're all characteristic of passion, which the dictionary defines as "a strong and barely controllable emotion." This powerful emotion can be expressed in unlimited ways, but are they all beneficial? Often, when pursuing either personal or professional goals, you're told to "follow your passion." That sounds natural, logical, inviting, and comfortable — even somewhat intriguing. But is it good advice, or not?

The Bible answers that question: *"It's fine to be zealous, provided the purpose is good."* (Galatians 4:18 NIV) The keyword is "purpose," something that's easily overlooked when you "follow your passion." Your passion, or zeal, comes from your heart. It's personal. Your passions are what excite you, what interests you, and what makes you happy. When it comes to passion, it's all about YOU. Passions are self-centered.

Self-centered, yes, but they're a huge motivator. You want to feel excited, interested, and happy; so you seek out and are attracted to activities that ignite your passions. That's natural; God designed you that way — but He wants more! He wants your passions to serve a purpose greater than just yourself: *"You shall love the Lord your God with all your heart and with all your soul and with all your mind. This is the great and first commandment. And a second is like it: You shall love your neighbor as yourself."* (Matt 22: 37-39 ESV)

Being self-centered, passion asks, "What can the world give me?" Whereas purpose asks, "What can I contribute to the world, or perhaps my neighbor?" Passion takes from the world; whereas, purpose involves both give and take: You take from the world what ignites and fuels your passion, but you give back by expending that passion-energy on goals that benefit others. Passion generates happiness, but that happiness is momentary. Purpose founded in Christ generates joy, and that joy is enduring.

Warning: Passions are attractive, often alluring, and have a strong, magnetic pull. If you "follow your passion" exclusively, it's possible to miss the big picture — to miss God's purpose for your life. You are more than just a packet of passions. The Master infused into you a unique set of gifts, talents and traits. The Bible says God will *equip you with all you need for doing His will.*" (Heb. 13:21 NLT) Notice the word "all." You'll need more than passion alone to discover and fulfill God's purpose for your life. Use all He has given you to paint your "big picture" — to create with your life the masterpiece God intended.

"God sees in you a masterpiece about to happen." (Max Lucado)

Think about it...

1. Name a time when your passion compelled you to "go the extra mile"?

2. What thoughts or activities always spark your passions?

3. What big goal do you have right now? Can you link a passion to that goal?

"Purpose is the reason you journey.
Passion is the fire that lights the way."

Anonymous

*"Never be afraid
to trust an unknown future
to a known God."*

Corrie ten Boom

Chapter 14

You Can Build a Brighter Future

You can create a better and brighter future because your view of your future has way more power than the memories of your past.

It may be true your classmates teased you in the 5th grade, or your mother loved your sister more than you, or your father abandoned you. It's possible your 9th-grade math teacher called you stupid, or

... human beings are the only creatures on earth that can take "what is" and make into something completely different.

you lived on the wrong side of the tracks, or you suffered serious traumatic events in your life such as sexual or physical abuse.

Such events are painful, and some are life-altering. Over time they accumulate deep within your soul and influence who and what you are today. However, you should never allow what happened in the past to determine your future. Here's why: you were created with the God-like quality of creativity.

Did you know that human beings are the only creatures on earth who can take "what is" and make it into something completely different? That's because we are made in the image of God, our Creator. We can take a plant and turn it into medicine. We can take sand and turn it into glass, or corn and turn it into gasoline. We can even take a single, harmless, invisible atom and create a cascading reaction — a dangerous nuclear bomb.

Let me repeat a phrase from the previous paragraph because it is so important: **You can take what is and make it into something completely different.**

The "what is" of your life is the reality of what happened in your past and the certainty of your present situation. Yet, how you got to where you are isn't nearly as important as where you are going. You are fully capable of creating a better and brighter future for yourself when you use the God-like creative power you already possess.

I experienced the reality of this truth when my wife of 52-years died of brain cancer. We were married as teenagers, so Amy and I grew up together. She was the only woman I ever loved, and life without her seemed empty. Like many who lose a loved one, I was

Define your future as God wants it to be.

forced to take "what is" and make it into something different. That's a challenge I've worked hard on since Amy's death, because living in the past would allow regrets to shape my future.

To be fully alive means to be fully present, and to do that you must leave the past in the past. The apostle Paul, who had much to regret, expressed this same thought: *"Forgetting what is behind and straining toward what is ahead, I press on toward the goal to win the prize for which God has called me heavenward in Christ Jesus."* (Phil. 3:13-14 NIV)

Like Paul, I want to press on. I want to be fully alive to meet my goals, and God wants that for me — and also for you. Day by day, I intentionally strive to live in the present and transform my life into a new creation. I find comfort knowing that, although Amy is gone, I am creating a new life. The love we shared will be forever in my heart — nestled there for those bittersweet moments when I choose to look within.

So, what does your future look like? Bright? Dim? Cloudy? Sunny? Happy? Sad?

Don't answer through the eyes of some national economic indicators. Don't respond through the colored lenses of past mistakes, or the tears of grievous loss. Answer, instead, through the eyes of your heart — looking outward to your hopes and dreams. Define your future as God wants it to be.

The majority of solutions emerge in your todays and tomorrows, not from your yesterdays. As you define your better, brighter future and work to create it, you won't have time to relive the blunders, insults, disappointments, and pain of yesterday. The power of your vision will enable you to take "what is" and create something completely different.

God has a special calling for you; discover it, define it, create it, and begin to live it today.

Think about it...

1. Were you teased, bullied, or called names in grade school or middle school?

2. Was there a teacher, coach, relative, or friend who took the time to help you grow into the person you are today?

3. Can you define what you want your future to look like?

*"Always be a first-rate version of yourself
and not a second-rate version
of someone else."*

Judy Garland

Chapter 15

You Can Be Fully You

When I was a kid, we had a 78-rpm record titled, "Little Orley: His Adventures as a Worm."

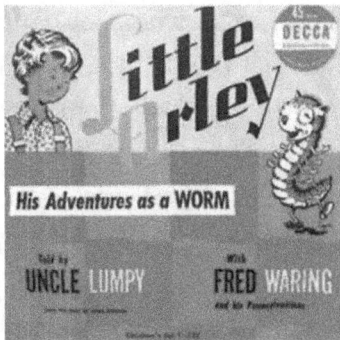

The story is about a little boy who worked in his father's cabbage field. As he worked, he observed that a cabbage worm never seemed to extend any effort; it just sat on a cabbage leaf, enjoyed the sun, and ate cabbage. So one day, Little Orley said, "Golly, I wish I was a cabbage worm!"

Just as Little Orley made his wish, he heard a big voice saying, "Little Orley, do you really want to be a cabbage worm?"

"I sure do," said Little Orley.

The big voice boomed back, "Then, Little Orley, be a cabbage worm!" And he was.

The rest of the story is about Little Orley's incredible and frightening adventures as a cabbage worm, which included the life-threatening dodges of a chef's knife in a fancy hotel kitchen.

The story ends when Little Orley realizes being Little Orley was a whole lot better than being a cabbage worm. He sighs, "I sure wish I was Little Orley again." The big voice answered, "Cabbage worm, be Little Orley." And he was.

Little Orley's story is a simple example of the scripture: *"All the toil of man is for his mouth, yet his appetite is not satisfied."* (Eccl. 6:7 ESV) The wisest man to live, Solomon wrote much about the futility, disappointments, and disillusions of life.

Like Little Orley, and much of humanity, you may not be able to answer two essential questions: "Who am I?" and "Why am I here?" With all his wealth, power, and wisdom, Solomon still grappled with those questions, so it's not surprising you would too.

Lacking answers to those eternal questions leaves you restless and discontented — in constant search of greener pastures — wanting more, but often more of the wrong thing for you. Like Little Orley, the grass might look greener on the other side of the fence. That greener vision appears frequently, and when it does ... BEWARE ... it might be AstroTurf!

The moral of the story is that only you can be you, and being the real you is the best thing you can do for yourself, for those closest to you, and for the rest of the world. Why? Because God created you unique,

No matter how old or young you are, it is not too late for you to be you.

genuine, and special — not a generic, contrived, imitation of something external. Therefore, you find greener grass (fulfillment) when you seek it from the One who knows you best, your Creator.

In case you've forgotten, the thesis of this book is this: You are not an accident; you are a special creation of God. In the 10,000-year history of humanity, there has never been anyone like you. Throughout millenniums to come, there will never be anyone like you again.

What does that mean? It means you are valuable beyond wealth; you are here for a reason; you are full of potential. No matter how young or old you are, it is never too late to be YOU. Give up on being a cabbage worm or whatever else it is that you or other people think you should be.

Ralph Waldo Emerson understood the war and peace of simply being yourself when he wrote, "To be yourself in a world that is constantly trying to make you something else is the greatest accomplishment."

Start today to be the unique, matchless, real YOU. Don't be content with the least you can be, be the most you can be. You're the only one who can be fully YOU because you're something special.

Think about it...

1. Have you ever felt like Little Orley?

2. Name at least one thing that makes you different from everyone else who has ever lived?

3. What "greener pastures" have pulled you in the wrong direction?

*"What the caterpillar
calls the end of the world,
the Master calls a butterfly."*

Richard Bach

Chapter 16

You're Full of Potential

"There is nothing in a caterpillar that tells you it's going to be a butterfly." (Richard Buckminster Fuller)

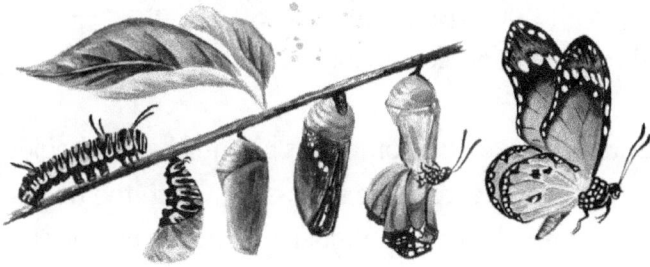

This sluggish creature's stubby legs and convoluted movement are the antitheses of the slender legs and weightless flutter of a graceful butterfly. You'd never know by looking that a caterpillar is born with everything it needs to become a butterfly. It is full of potential, all hidden within a tiny egg the size of a pinhead.

Although it reads like science fiction, a butterfly's inconceivable life cycle (egg, larva, pupa, adult) is a true story. It's an awesome and inspiring story with four short chapters:

Chapter One: This is the shortest chapter in a butterfly's life cycle — the *egg stage of life*. It begins when a butterfly lays an egg on a leaf. In a few days, a tiny, almost invisible creature within the egg starts to feast on the eggshell, and soon our main character has eaten his way out of the shell. He instinctively knows his purpose in life — to eat and grow — so he immediately proceeds to gorge on the leaf.

Chapter Two: This somewhat boring chapter begins with an escape from the shell, after which the minuscule caterpillar eats continually for about two weeks. The tiny creature grows 100 times its size during this *larva stage of life*. As he grows, his skin splits and molts several times before finally forming a chrysalis (referred to as a cocoon for a moth), a protective hard shell within which a butterfly forms.

Chapter Three: This surreal chapter begins with formation of the chrysalis, described above, and is all about the mind-blowing *pupa stage of life*. Many people think that inside the chrysalis the caterpillar simply grows wings and then flies away. It's not that simple; in fact, the transformation that occurs isn't simple at all.

"... all of the body tissue is digested into a soupy goo."

The complexity of this metamorphosis might best be described as "awesome," a word that can mean both awful and awe-inspiring. Synonyms for awesome range from magnificent to terrible, from beautiful to horrifying. Indeed, the transformation that occurs in the chrysalis is awesome — so awesome, if the caterpillar knew what he was in for, he might have second thoughts about hosting the event!

As the unsuspecting creature hangs upside down, resting in his chrysalis, a surge of enzymes flood his body. Every cell self-destructs, and all of the body tissue is digested into a soupy "goo" — all except for the special "imaginal discs," which were present from the beginning when the caterpillar was still in the egg.

> *"Your blueprint includes a powerful mind with an unlimited imagination."*

You might describe this carnage in the chrysalis as terrible, dreadful, or horrifying, and any caterpillar would probably agree. This meltdown sounds awful, not awe-inspiring. But keep reading because Chapter Three gets much better ...

Seemingly out of nowhere, dormant imaginal discs awaken and rapidly produce new imaginal cells, fueled by the nutrient-rich soup surrounding them. These cells grow independently at first, forming various body parts — wings, legs, eyes, antennae —but eventually grow together to form a butterfly.

Chapter Four: This delightful chapter is devoted to the *adult stag*e of life when, like magic, a fully developed butterfly emerges from its chrysalis. After hanging in place just long enough to dry his wings, the delicate butterfly flutters away to mate and lay eggs. And then the story repeats. How awesome is that!

The butterfly is a powerful symbol of both transformation and potential. From conception in the egg through the caterpillar stage of life, the extraordinary "imaginal discs" are present but dormant. Those slumbering discs hold incredible potential. They are the blueprint for an awesome project — the construction of a butterfly from a soupy goo.

If God can construct a butterfly out of caterpillar-goo, think what he can make out of you! Like a butterfly, you too have a blueprint for construction. Encoded in your DNA since conception are gifts, talents, and abilities, along with interests, passions, and personality traits — a totally unique blend of everything needed to fulfill your purpose in life. The Bible says God *"equips you with everything good for doing ... what is pleasing to Him."* (Hebrews 13:21 NIV)

You may not have imaginal discs to awaken, but your blueprint includes a powerful mind with an unlimited imagination. Transformation begins when you awaken those — when you thoughtfully consider and use what God has written in your DNA, inscribed in your heart, and instructed in His Word. You're full of potential, much more potential than you can realize. Awaken it, use it, and start to imagine God's special plan for your life.

Think about it...

1. Think of a personal transformation that you have experienced.

2. What sparked your transformation and what did you learn from the experience?

3. How are you using your "unique blend" of talents and passions that God gave you.

"There is no greater discovery than seeing God as the author of your destiny."

Ravi Zacharias

"How does one become a butterfly?
You have to want to learn to fly so much
that you are willing to give up
being a caterpillar."

Unknown

Chapter 17

You're Under Construction

"Every human being is under construction from conception to death." (Billy Graham)

Like a caterpillar that goes through transformation to become a butterfly, your life goes through stages of construction and transformation also. Once in awhile, a caterpillar doesn't build a chrysalis; thus, he evades the total "meltdown" and metamorphosis that occurs in the pupa stage of life. But in doing so, he forever forfeits the opportunity to fly.

> *It's easy to get stuck in the caterpillar stage of life.*

Standstills like this happen with people too. For whatever reason — wealth, fame, lust, pride, comfort, pain, depression, fear, etc. — it's possible to stop growing for awhile, sometimes a very long while. It's easy to get stuck in the caterpillar stage of life. For Vance Johnson, former Denver Bronco star and one of the "Three Amigos," the reason was addiction.

> *"I had to be completely broken before I was ready for what God intended."*
>
> *Vance Johnson*

In his book, "*UNCOVERED – Why Becoming Less Became Everything,*" this popular three-time Super Bowl player candidly shares his powerful, near-death story. Vance came to realize, "I had to be completely broken before I was ready for what God intended."

Like a caterpillar in its chrysalis, it took a total meltdown before Vance eventually surrendered his old life of addiction to rebuild anew: "You can find a new purpose and life and restore all that you have lost. Maybe in a different way, but a more fulfilling and enriching way."

Vance reveals, "Every step I've taken in my life was ordained to bring me to where I am now." Just as a loving parent instructs his child, so God orders your life to teach you, to build character, to strengthen faith, and, ultimately, to save you.

Some lessons are incredibly painful, but necessary, if you are to move beyond the caterpillar stage of life and experience inner transformation. As the Bible says, *"No discipline seems pleasant at the time, but painful. Later on, however, it produces a harvest of righteousness and peace for those who have been trained by it."* (Hebrews 12:11 NIV)

Billy Graham taught, "Each life is made of mistakes and learning, waiting and growing, practicing patience and being persistent." Life is about learning, growth, and change; God planned it that way. Every experience and every challenge is a test — an opportunity to learn, to build character and faith, and to be transformed. The more difficult the test, the greater the potential for learning and growth.

Sometimes difficulties seem overwhelming, even paralyzing, but rest assured, "God never wastes a painful experience." (Rick Warren) Transformation is a gradual process that changes you little by little,

"... into a new person. You were created to be like God, truly righteous and holy." (Eph. 4:24 CEV)

You know what the transformation of a caterpillar looks like: a butterfly. It's a win-win for the caterpillar, who not only trades awkward for elegant but also receives the gift of flight. But what will your transformation look like? You want and need to know.

> *"One can never consent to creep when one feels an impulse to soar."*
>
> Helen Keller

The Bible makes it clear you were created in the image of God, to be the visible image of God. However, nobody has seen God; and words alone, i.e., almighty, benevolent, holy, loving, powerful, worthy, seem abstract and often yield more questions than answers. God wants no confusion. He wants you to see and understand your goal clearly, to know precisely what transformation looks like. Therefore, he gave you a visual: *"Christ, who is the exact likeness of God."* (2 Cor. 4:4 GNT) Jesus is what your transformation looks like.

"We delight in the beauty of a butterfly, but rarely admit the changes it has to go through to achieve that beauty." (Maya Angelou) Such butterfly-beauty is external, but it starts internally during metamorphosis. So, too, does your transformation originate within. It starts in your mind: *"Do not conform to the pattern of this world, but be transformed by the renewing of your mind. Then you will be able to test and approve what God's will is — his good, pleasing and perfect will."* (Rom. 12:2 NIV) Your mind is renewed and you grow in wisdom as you apply God's word to your life experiences.

"One can never consent to creep when one feels an impulse to soar." These words came from Helen Keller, who lived in a dark and silent world. Because you're made in the image of God, you too have that same impulse to soar. It's part of your blueprint; it's encoded in your DNA. You're packed with potential, and your life is a construction project that requires endless change, boundless endurance, and growing faith. It's a magnificent, life-long project — a beautiful transformation God wants to complete in you because He's always known ***You're Something Special!***

Think about it ...

1. Describe the most difficult challenges you've faced in life.

2. How did these experiences transform you?

3. God knows you're something special. Do you?

"It is finished."

Jesus

AFFIRMATIONS OF A SPECIAL PERSON

This, I believe:

I believe that within me is an inexhaustible supply of God-given potential. I believe I have

> More **intelligence** than I have ever used
> More **creativity** than I have ever imagined
> More **courage** than I have ever exhibited
> More **faith** than I have ever relied upon
> More **joy** than I have ever felt
> More **love** than I have ever known
> More **peace** than I have ever presumed
> More **passion** than I have ever experienced
> More **endurance** than I have ever summoned
> More **success** than I have ever thought possible

I believe I can **solve** problems,
> **overcome** obstacles,
>> and **achieve** goals.

With God's help and my commitment to fulfilling His purpose for my life, I shall succeed.

This, I believe!

AFTERWORD

A Special Message for Grandparents

This book is dedicated to grandchildren everywhere. That's because Ron and Carol (the authors) think their grandchildren are something special. Don't you think your grandkids are the best and brightest children ever? Of course, you do; that's why you call them "grand!"

And it works both ways. For many kids there are no people on earth as special and understanding as their grandparents. An Italian proverb makes the point: "If nothing is going well, call your grandma."

As your grandkids grow, you post pictures on Facebook and get magnetic frames for your refrigerator. You stick "World's Best Grandpa" and "Proud Grandma" bumper stickers on your cars. You proudly attend ball games and dance recitals, and you never miss a birthday.

As they grow up and you grow older, you sense a heartfelt yearning to impart to your grandchildren what matters most in life — to leave a legacy of love. You not only think about Christmas and birthday gifts but also seek ways to share your wisdom, experience, and understanding about life. This means when you come to your grandchildren with gifts, some of the most valuable and enduring gifts will likely be intangible. Now you offer gifts of the heart — three gifts: (1) the gift of wisdom and understanding, (2) the gift of perspective, and (3) the gift of real-life stories.

You want to give **the gift of wisdom and understanding.** You know your grandchildren will face a thousand-thousand decisions, temptations, and opportunities; and you want to prepare them for the difficult choices ahead. Grandma and Grandpa realize, *"How much better to get wisdom than gold! To get understanding is to be chosen rather than silver."* (Proverbs 16:16 ESV) You yearn to share all you've learned with your grandchildren.

You also want to give **the gift of perspective.** Young children are impulsive and filled with uninhibited excitement. Teenagers face temptations and physical changes that confuse them. Young adults make decisions based on little experience but filled with hope.

Grandparents know almost in detail what changes and challenges their offspring will face. You know it because you lived it. You see the lives of your grandchildren from the perspective of time — not a moment of time, but a generation of time. You long to help your grandchildren through the bumps and detours of life.

You want to give **the gift of real-life stories**, parables from the experiences of life. The psalmist understood the value of real-life stories: *"I'll let you in on the sweet old truths, stories we heard from our fathers, counsel we learned at our mother's knee. We're not keeping this to ourselves; we're passing it along to the next generation."* (Pslm. 78:2-4 Msg) You harbor an abundance of intriguing and valuable real-life stories you want very much to share.

You have yearnings to leave a legacy of love because God knows something about grandparents, something the world often misses: *"Wisdom belongs to the aged, and understanding to those who have lived many years."* (Job 12:12 NLT)

God recognizes the enduring value of your wisdom, experience, and understanding. Therefore, He assigns you a unique and powerful role in the lives of your grandchildren: *"Stay vigilant as long as you live. Teach what you've seen and heard to your children and grandchildren."* (Deut. 4:9 Msg).

The Bible doesn't say to send little ones to public school to learn history; nor does it say to hire a youth leader to explain the difference between good and evil. God knows teachers and leaders aren't always worthy of our trust. The Bible directs grandparents: You do it — you who lived it, you who learned it, you who felt it, you who fought for it — you tell the children. Tell them personally, tell them often, and tell them in as many ways you can. Remind your young of who they are, from whence they have come, and why they are here.

Who better to teach a child that God is Creator of the universe than a godly grandma? Who better to defend the biblical foundation of America than a grandpa who knows the price of freedom? Who better to reflect God's presence in the human heart than loving grandparents?

In America today, God is suppressed, constitutional rights are canceled, truth is exchanged for lies, and our youth are deceived. This leaves seniors concerned for the legacy their children and grandchildren will inherit. Ronald Reagan warned, "Freedom is a fragile thing and is never more than one generation away from extinction." Seniors worry if freedom and the blessings of a God-centered life will be perpetuated.

"Young people need something stable to hang on to — a culture connection, a sense of their own past, a hope for their own future. Most of all, they need what grandparents can give them." (Jay Kesler)

Ron and Carol invite you to learn about a love-inspired, national movement of concerned seniors who lift youth with truth and amplify the awareness of God. Visit PowerfulSeniors.com, where you will find a growing library of resources designed to inspire and empower you to connect with your grandchildren in fun and meaningful ways.

POWERFUL SENIORS

Lifting Youth with Truth

In America today, God is suppressed, constitutional rights are canceled, truth is exchanged for lies, and our youth are deceived. This leaves many seniors concerned for the legacy their children and grandchildren will inherit. Through an online library of resources, **Powerful Seniors** empowers seniors to amplify the awareness of God — God in creation, God in America, and God in every human heart. This ever-expanding force of committed seniors perpetuates freedom and the blessings of a God-centered life.

Our Vision: A love-inspired, national movement of concerned seniors who lift youth with truth and amplify the awareness of God. This ever-expanding force faithfully fulfills God's commission for seniors: *"Stay vigilant as long as you live. Teach what you've seen and heard to your children and grandchildren."* (Deut. 4:9 Msg)

PowerfulSeniors.com

ONLY YOU CAN BE YOU

Only you can be you,
Only I can be me.
When we are who we are,
We are really set free.

So let's you and I
Do all we can do;
First I'll improve me,
While you shape up you.

And when our life's done,
We'll know we were true,
I was uniquely me;
You were matchlessly you.

Ron Ross

About the Authors

Ronald D. Ross, B.A., D.Min., D.Th.

After growing up in a parsonage, Dr. Ross served as pastor, missionary to Africa, marriage seminar leader, author, publisher, and more. Most of those 60+ years, he was accompanied by his wife, who died of brain cancer in 2015. Together, they traveled the world, raised three children, and now have four grandchildren and two great-grandchildren.

The books he wrote over the years reveal his interest in a variety of subjects, for example: *How to Record Your Family History* (three editions), *Handbook for Citizen Journalists, Confidence When You Need It the Most,* and *Trivia Pop Quiz.* He authored three books on marriage: *Keep Mama Happy, It's About Us,* and *7 Assumptions About Marriage.* His latest book, *You're Something Special,* is based on a popular series of newspaper columns he wrote.

Dr. Ross had the privilege of working with the late-great radio newsman, Paul Harvey. He had personal interviews with two presidents: Gerald R. Ford, in his retirement home in Beaver Creek, Colo., and Kenneth Kaunda, president of Zambia.

Dr. Ross is a founding partner of *Powerful Seniors,* an online organization directed to the hearts and lives of active seniors who want to leave a legacy of love for their descendants. He says, "With God's help, this last chapter of my life will be the best chapter of all."

An award-winning, dynamic speaker, Dr. Ross lives in Loveland, Colorado.

Contact: Dr.Ross@YoureSomethingSpecial.com

Carol E. Hall, B.A.

Carol's earliest memories include attending Sunday school with her twin sister, Sue, at the First Presbyterian Church in Hot Springs, Arkansas. In matching attire —down to the patent leather shoes and little white gloves — these tiny tots marched into church every Sunday morning, always holding hands. In 1962 at age 15, their high school youth group traveled to Montreat-Anderson College in Montreat, North Carolina for a special summer camp focused on vocational aptitude testing. Carol still recalls the highlight of that week: In an overflowing campus chapel, Reverend Billy Graham delivered a powerful message worded precisely for teens. Many surrendered their lives to Christ, and Dr. Graham's message profoundly impacted Carol and her twin.

Those early aptitude tests pointed Carol toward a vocation in engineering; however, her creative passions won the tug of war, and she graduated with a BA in Commercial Art from the University of Arkansas. It was the right choice. After college Carol married and had two children. To satisfy her creative yen, she taught the age-old art of porcelain painting, which eventually morphed into a full-time business. Through this venture, Artistic Tile, Carol created custom murals for homes along the Colorado Front Range.

After years of painting, Carol broadened her path. Hoping to combine her artistic talent and education with new technology — the Apple Macintosh — she enrolled in a 2-year computer graphics program. A perfect match! As the first generation Mac evolved, so did Carol's graphic design career, which led her to co-found Pixelink, LLC, an advertising agency where she served clients as a designer and editor. After 30 years in advertising, Carol retired ... or so she thought.

Then, in 2018, Carol met Ron Ross at a Bible study and quickly realized they share many common interests and experiences. Both cherish their children and grandchildren, a passion that led Carol and Ron to co-found Powerful Seniors. Carol lives in Loveland, Colorado. Her blessings are many, but at the top of the list are two special children and two very special grandchildren ... and, naturally, one very similar identical twin.

Contact: CarolHall@YoureSomethingSpecial.com

Resources

Books

Become the Best Version of Yourself, by Billy Arcement
21 undeniable lessons to create the best version of yourself

The Light Within Me, by Ainsley Earhardt
A personal story of how faith inspired achievement and supported the author through trying times

Cultivate Courage, by Dave Cornell
Practical actionable steps to face your fears and lead a more courageous life

Uncovered, by Vance Johnson
The author's personal story of the destruction brought on by addiction and the power of faith in finding his way back from the depths of hell

Cure for the Common Life, by Max Lucado
Practical tools for exploring and identifying your uniqueness, and the perfect prescription for finding and living in your sweet spot for the rest of your life

The Purpose Driven Life, by Rick Warren
Spiritual principles that offer guidelines to focus your energy, simplify your decisions, give your life meaning — and prepare you for eternity

You're Something Special by Ron Ross & Carol Hall
is available on Amazon.com. For a quick link and more
information, visit https://YoureSomethingSpecial.com/

Other Resources

Gaither Music: https://Gaither.com/
One of the world's largest and most popular independent
Christian music companies and a household name for mil-
lions of gospel music fans

Grandkids Matter: https://GrandKidsMatter.org/
A clearinghouse of information that brings top-notch
resources and insights to grandparents

Human Coalition: https://HumanCoalition.org/
A champion of life committed to an audacious mission: to
transform our culture of death into a culture of life — to
end abortion in America

Discover Jesus: https://Jesus.net/
An international network of more than 40 partners united
to make disciples of Christ through innovative and creative
websites and online tools

How to become a Christian: https://PeaceWithGod.net
Find peace with God at this website operated by the Billy
Graham Evangelistic Association.

OTHER BOOKS BY DR. ROSS

How to Record Your Family History

If you want to leave a legacy of love for future gener-ations, this book is the place to begin. Today's technology makes it is easier than ever to preserve family stories using audio, video, and written for-mats. Dr. Ross wrote this book after his experience of recording both vid-eo and audio stories told by his par-ents. The book is available in Kindle or printed format. For information visit RecordYourFamilyHistory.com.

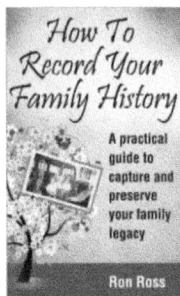

IT'S ABOUT US!
Marriage: What we do to get what we want for each other

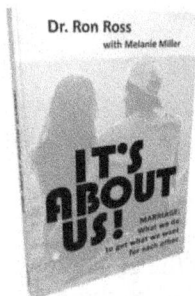

Drawing on his Christian worldview and a fulfilling 52-year marriage, Dr. Ross authors sixteen chapters of fascinating insights and practical, actionable items that are sure to refresh your marriage. The book is available in Kindle or print. For more information visit: ItsAboutUsBook.com.

Seven Assumptions About Marriage

In this book, Dr. Ron Ross defines his seven assumptions about marriage in a simple, straight-forward way, showing his Christian worldview in the process. Marriage is intended to be something wonderful, something good, something to be treasured by individuals, couples, families, and communities until death-do-us-part. Available on Amazon:

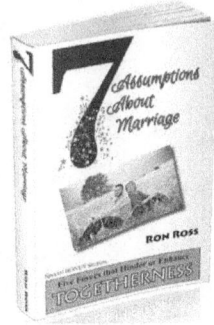

https://www.amazon.com/dp/B01N9VRUG5/

Confidence When You Need It the Most

Dr. Ross writes, "Confident people have natural magnetism and are immediately identified when they enter a room. They walk with buoyancy, stand with dignity, speak with conviction, and love with passion. They believe in their abilities to solve problems, overcome obstacles, and achieve goals. Confident people inspire trust and gain the support and loyalty of their families, friends, bosses, clients, and even strangers."
Visit: ConfidenceWhenYouNeedIt.com

"Go after a life of love as if your life depended on it — because it does. Give yourselves to the gifts God gives you."

1 Corinthians 14:1 Msg

www.ingramcontent.com/pod-product-compliance
Lightning Source LLC
LaVergne TN
LVHW021458080426
835509LV00018B/2334